New York's 50 Best

Places to Find Peace and Quiet

Third Edition

Allan Ishac

Universe • New York

Acknowledgments
In many ways this is a peculiar little book, a compendium of
peaceful places within a metropolis known for its nonstop
action, energy, and fast living. It takes a publisher with sensitivity to the quieter sides of our city to appreciate what this
book offers, and to keep it successfully in print for a decade.
For that, I thank Helene Silver at City & Company, who has
achieved her vision of creating valuable books about every
aspect of New York for those of us who love this city. I also
extend my gratitude to the many enthusiastic staffers at City &
Company who nurtured this book over the years; especially
my editor, Andrea DiNoto, whose red pencil made me cringe,
but whose skill and gentle manner made me listen.
Thank you all.

First Universe edition published in the United States of America
in 2003
by UNIVERSE PUBLISHING
a Division of Rizzoli International Publications, Inc.
300 Park Avenue South
New York, NY 10010

© 1991, 1995, 1997, 2001, 2003 by Allan Ishac
Previously published by City and Company
Interior Design by Don Wise & Co., based on an original design
by Nancy Steiny
Cover Design: Paul Kepple and Jude Buffum @ Headcase Design
Cover Illustration by Mary Lynn Blasutta

2003 2004 2005 2006 2007 / 10 9 8 7 6 5 4 3 2 1
Third Edition
Printed in the United States
Library of Congress Catalog Control Number: 2002111641
ISBN# 0-7893-0834-7

Publisher's Note: Neither Universe Publishing nor the author
has any interest, financial or personal, in the locations listed in
this book. While every effort was made to ensure that all data
was accurate at the time of publication, we advise calling
ahead or checking Web sites to confirm details.

All phone number are area code 212 unless otherwise noted.

Dedication

To all New Yorkers, who have lived through a heart-breaking tragedy, and who now, more than ever, need the solace of sanctuaries, the refuge of serene retreats, the quiet found in stillness.

Contents

Preface

Some years ago, as I lay in that vague twilight between waking and sleeping, ten words flashed like teletype across the black screen of my closed eyelids: "25 Places To Find Peace And Quiet In New York." End of transmission.

I sat up quickly, suddenly wide awake. What was that, I wondered? Some sort of cryptic message from my unconscious? I scribbled the words on a scrap of paper by my bed, and for the next six months this crumpled communique kept popping up around me, seeming to demand my attention.

At that time, I had been planning to leave New York, feeling overwhelmed by its noise, pace, and general tensions. That's when it struck me, the words of a thousand prophets — "you teach what you most need to learn." The message was clear: I needed to learn how to find peace and quiet in the midst of all the chaos. Those ten little words, I realized,

were the title of a book, and I was sup-
posed to write it.

So I did. I published the guide myself,
hoping to sell my initial fifteen hundred
copies through mail order. Within weeks
of publication, a series of serendipitous
events occurred. First, my little book
found its way onto the desk of a major
bookstore buyer, who promptly ordered
five hundred copies. Then, an enthusiastic literary agent agreed to represent me.
Soon after, she was called by a publisher
who was interested in an expanded edition. My head was pleasantly spinning.

I wrestle with ideas about divine guid-
ance, and I am not someone who knows
the name of his personal angel. But I do
know that the experience of writing this
book has changed my life. And I find
myself saying to whoever "typed" those
first simple words inside my head, "Do
it again and this time I won't wait six
months to get the message."

Allan Ishac

Introduction

Since 1990, this little book has helped thousands of New Yorkers find places of serenity and solitude in our noisy, over-crowded city. Its subject, peace and quiet, are qualities of life I not only crave, I believe they are essential to good health and a happy mind.

But in a city that offers "everything," peace and quiet are rare commodities indeed. It is difficult to find even a moment's relief from the cacophony of assaulting sounds: shrieking car horns, incessant cell phones, clattering garbage trucks, noisy neighbors, the rumble of the subway, the scream of urgent sirens. New Yorkers try to tune out this offen-sive din, but the effort exacts a heavy toll. Noise, more ubiquitous than any pollution we face in this city, can make us tired, irritable — and even ill. So how can we stay and still get away? As the consummate serenity seeker, I ask myself this question all the time. In *New York's 50 Best Places to Find Peace and Quiet* I provide the answer.

The release of this edition of my book coincides with the one-year anniversary of the September 11th catastrophe. It seems to me that now, more than ever, we need access to urban sanctuaries that offer solace, refuge, and relaxation. Among those I've included, some are outdoors; some are in; and some are in between. Some charge a fee; most are free. What they all have in common is that they offer rest and retreat — a refreshing dip into an oasis of quiet.

I hope you will carry this guide with you in your briefcase, backpack, or handbag and use it when you need to escape to a tranquil place — whether for just a minute, or an hour, during your otherwise hectic day.

Alley's End
Restaurant

Address: 311 W. 17th St. bet 8th and 9th Aves.
Phone: 627-8899
Hours: Nightly, 6 P.M. to 11 P.M.,
Weekends until 1 A.M.
Admission: Entrees from $15
Subway: A, C, E to 14th St.; 1, 9 to 18th St.
Bus: M11 (Ninth and Tenth Aves.) to 18th St.

When I do speaking engagements for this book, I'm always asked about quiet places to dine. In so many of today's city restaurants, poor acoustics, intrusive sound systems and loud patrons are a constant irritation. It's often impossible to have a casual conversation without straining the vocal chords. So I went out seeking establishments that offer a modicum of serenity.

Alley's End is just such a place. While most restaurants covet a high-visibility location, owners Judy and Richard Kingman wanted their Chelsea place to be hidden away and hard-to-find (look for the inconspicuous fork-and-knife neon above the front gate). The remote, end-of-the-alley location is your first clue that you're not destined for the usual high-decibel dinner.

Step inside Alley's End and you'll experience its subdued charm instantly. The comfortable neighborhood bistro is known for its spot-lit, glass-enclosed central garden. With a tiny pond and trickling fountain, this patch of wild forest brings the stillness of the outdoors in, and offers diners a serene point of focus. Ask for a table in the romantic "greenhouse" room and you'll enjoy excellent American cuisine while overlooking this soothing nature scene.

A diner's right to quiet conversation is respected at these eateries, too: Paola's (245 E. 84th Street, 794-1890) serves the city's freshest pasta in peace at their low-key, side street restaurant. The mellow Lhasa Restaurant (96 Second Avenue at 5th Street, 674-5870) has fine Tibetan food, tranquil music and an outdoor rock garden.

Astor Court
at the Met

Address: Metropolitan Museum of Art,
Fifth Ave. and 82nd St.
Phone: 535-7710
Hours: Tuesday through Thursday and Sunday,
9:30 A.M. to 5:30 P.M.; Friday and Saturday,
9:30 A.M. to 9 P.M.; closed Monday
Admission: $10 suggested donation
Subway: 4, 5, 6 to 86th St., walk west
Bus: M1, 2, 3, 4, 5 to 82nd St.

brooke Astor spent part of her childhood in Beijing, where I like to imagine she would play hide-and-seek in Chinese courtyards. What other explanation could there be for Astor Court — a flawlessly recreated Ming Dynasty scholar's garden which was conceived and funded by the renowned philanthropist especially for the Metropolitan Museum of Art. Perhaps Mrs. Astor was seeking a grown-up place to hide during those gala museum events held in her honor.

It is an unspoken rule of the Met that this refined environment retains its sanctuary-like qualities. Thus, voices are lowered, cameras are pocketed, and visitors wander the covered walkways in a state of reverie and respect.

Meant for the contemplation of nature, the courtyard contains a rock garden, Chinese plantings, a trickling waterfall, and a goldfish pool. A tinted glass dome over the court simulates the sky and suggests its traditional use as an open-air moon-viewing terrace in its native setting. Even on the sunniest days, the installation is cast in a diffused, dreamy twilight.

Garden courtyards in China were often given poetic names by their scholar owners. This one, appropriately enough, is called "In Search of Quietude."

Note: Two other Met destinations afford ample repose. The Temple of Dendur in the Egyptian wing is almost eerily quiet. Seasonally, you can also enjoy the Cantor Roof Garden on the fifth floor, part wood deck and stone terrace offering dramatic views of Central Park.

Atmananda Yoga & Holistic Center

Address: 552 Broadway at Spring St., 3rd Floor
Phone: 625-1511
Hours: Monday through Friday, 8 A.M. to 10
P.M., Saturday and Sunday,
10 A.M. to 5 P.M. Call for class schedule
Admission: Classes begin at $14
Subway: N or R to Prince St.; 6 to Spring St.
Bus: M1, 6 (Broadway) to Spring St.
Web site: www.atmananda.com

Yoga, by definition, is a meditative practice, so you might think all yoga studios would be places for focused, quiet contemplation. But it actually took me years to find a yoga center suitable for this book — one that consistently enveloped me in a sense of serenity, comfort and calm.

This quality of gentle stillness was apparent at Atmananda the first time I walked in to take a beginner's class. The staff was genuinely friendly and welcoming, and eager to introduce me to yoga's rejuvenating qualities. The hushed atmosphere is entirely pleasant and the sweet fragrance of the Nag Champa incense (typically burned in

14

Tibetan Buddhist temples) blessed the air with a sacred solemnity.

Atmananda, which means "spiritual bliss" in Sanskrit, is situated in a former nineteenth century SoHo warehouse with ancient brick walls and 160-year-old wood floors whose burnished patina seems to sustain yoga practice. The center includes two yoga rooms, a meditation area, a Pilates studio and holistic treatment rooms, where a wide variety of services for body, mind and soul are offered.

Personally, I value the gentle, stress-reducing benefits of my twice-weekly yoga classes (a combination of Ashtanga, Iyengar, and Hatha styles). The knowledgeable instructors are compassionate and encouraging, the breathing techniques energize me, and the slow asanas (postures) stretch my body and increase my flexibility. I'm no yogi yet, but at Atmananda they're very patient.

Yoga Lover's Note: I also found excellent instruction and a tranquil atmosphere at Kundalini Yoga East (873 Broadway, 982-5959).

Bartow-Pell Mansion Museum

Address: 895 Shore Road, Bronx
Phone: (718) 885-1461
Hours: Museum open Wednesday,
Saturday and Sunday, Noon to 4 P.M.;
Grounds open Tuesday through Sunday,
8:30 A.M. to 4:30 P.M.
Admission: $2.50 for museum tour;
free to grounds
Subway: 6 to Pelham Bay stop,
then take bus below
Bus: 45 Westchester-Bee Line to gates
(no bus Sundays)
Auto: Call for directions

every now and then, I contract a serious case of "urbanitis," for which I know only one cure — trees, grass, open space. And lots of it. On those days, when even Central Park lacks adequate healing power, I head to the Bartow-Pell Mansion in the Bronx, where I can find ample doses of the much-needed antidotes.

Although located near the Westchester border, Bartow-Pell is surprisingly accessible. Peering up the winding drive into wooded estate grounds from the massive mansion gates, I am always filled with a splendid anticipation of the country elegance lying just ahead.

The mansion, one of the finest examples of early Greek Revival architecture in America, is famous for its seashell shaped, three-story hanging stair-case, a gravity-defying marvel of construction. The self-guided tour includes a visit to a pleasant "orangerie"— a French-style greenhouse room — where strong southern light warms the chilliest of winter days.

Outside, explore the mansion's nine-and-a-half rolling acres, including walled formal gardens with lawns that spill seamlessly into nearby Long Island Sound. The urbanitis cure reaches full potency after I've walked the property's well-marked paths through virgin forests and marsh-lands, or venture onto the bordering Siwanoy Hiking Trail through more than two thousand acres of Pelham Bay Park. Got a case of urbani-tis? Take two hours of undisturbed hiking and call me in the morning.

The Boathouse in Central Park

Address: Enter at 72nd St. and Fifth Ave.,
travel 200 yards north
Phone: 517-2233
Hours: Monday through Friday, 10:30 A.M. to
5:30 P.M.; Saturday and Sunday,
10 A.M. to 6 P.M. (seasonal)
Admission: $10 per hour per boat
(seats up to five)
Subway: 6 to 68th St., walk west
Bus: M1, 2, 3, 4 (Fifth and Madison Aves.
to 72nd St.)

You're skimming over tranquil waters, passing under a quaint wooden footbridge. You see a flock of water birds take flight in the distance as another rowboat emerges from a reed bed nearby. Is this a fishing pond in Maine? An unexplored inlet off Chesapeake Bay? Would you believe the Central Park lake?

Native New Yorkers often mistakenly think of this picturesque urban refuge as overcrowded and, frankly, too touristy. While the Central Park lake does draw large crowds on weekends, it offers weekday visitors a unique and inexpensive way to escape the city without ever leaving it. Purchase your ticket at the fast-food counter of the Loeb Boathouse Cafeteria. Courteous attendants will then assist you with oars (and requisite life jacket), and set you off in a rowboat. Wherever you can row you can go, and with more than eighteen acres of open water and side pools, you can go far.

This is one place where I guarantee you won't be bugged or bothered, badgered or bullied. Which is reason enough to go row.

Traveler's Note: The romantically inclined can inquire at the Loeb Boathouse about spring and summer gondola rides on the lake ($30 for a half-hour).

Carapan

**Address: 5 West 16th St., garden level, bet.
Fifth and Sixth Aves.
Phone: 633-6220
Hours: Daily, 10 A.M. to 9:45 P.M. by appt.
Admission: 60 to 70-minute sessions, $95
Subway: 4, 5, 6, N, R to Union Square
Bus: M2, 3, 4, 5 (Fifth Ave.) to 16th St.
Web site: www.carapan.com**

It may cost you a little more for the peace and quiet they offer at Carapan, but to me, it is worth the price.

A place to go for bodywork, both esoteric and familiar, Carapan offers everything from Swedish massage and shiatsu to aromatherapy and natural herbal face treatments. I can tell you from first-hand (pun intended) experience that the massage practitioners here are highly skilled, with special attention given to those parts of the body — feet, neck and shoulders, for example — especially vulnerable to Big City stress. I can also assure you that you will return to Carapan as much for the healing atmosphere as the healing arts.

At Carapan, you feel embraced by the revitalizing effects and calming energy of the Southwest, which they have perfectly evoked here. As the subtle scents of juniper, piñon, and mesquite incense permeate the rooms, soothing music plays, and you are sensually transported from gritty Greenwich Village to the mesas of Sante Fe. Carapan's retail store evokes the spirit of the region, too, with an intriguing assortment of Native American offerings from sage smudge sticks to feathered "dream catchers."

Carapan calls itself a tranquil place where you can go to restore your spirit. I call it that and much more. Even if you don't go for the body-work, stop by just to inhale.

Cherry Walk at the Hudson River

Address: 100th St. to 125th St. Enter Riverside
Park at 98th St., walk west to the river
Phone: 1-800-201-PARK
Hours: Seven days, Dawn to dusk
Admission: Free
Subway: 1, 9 to 96th St, walk five minutes
west
Bus: M5, M104 to 100th St.

Consecrated by the feet of a hundred thousand serenity-seekers. That's how I think of Cherry Walk, the narrow ribbon of land that meanders along the Hudson River between 100th and 125th Streets.

For decades, the ambling masses have been so devoted to this simple but seductive footpath that the Parks Department finally decided to make it official. In 2000 the city tastefully and artistically paved the single track of dirt and christened it Cherry Walk, in honor of the diminutive cherry trees that explode with blossom and fragrance along both sides of the Henry

Hudson Parkway in the spring.

Sensitive landscape architects have managed to preserve all the grace this shoulder of grass and trees has to offer. Not more than 30 feet wide in most places, the macadam walkway serpentines between trees and quarried granite boulders, which have been strategically placed for intermittent rest stops and river contemplation. At the shoreline, massive flat stones slope gently toward the water and provide an inviting place to remove shoes or roller-blades and lean back to face the sun. All the while, the tidal surge licks and laps at your feet.

Despite its proximity to the highway, Cherry Walk seems remarkably insulated from the traffic — you can easily saunter along, oblivious to the passing cars. People who have loved this hospitable path since it was just a rutted trail have always known this. Now you can make that pleasant discovery, too.

The Cloisters

Address: Northern tip of Fort Tryon Park
Phone: 923-3700
Hours: Tuesday through Sunday,
9:30 A.M. to 5:15 P.M.
Admission: $10 suggested donation
Subway: A to 190th St., walk 10 minutes north
Bus: M4 directly to The Cloisters
Auto: Henry Hudson Pkwy. north to first exit
after George Washington Bridge

i was running along a treacherous rampart, chased by a frothing gargoyle. I came to the arched doorway of a remote abbey where I was offered refuge by … an employee of the Metropolitan Museum of Art!

This was no dream; just vivid imagery from a recent trip to The Cloisters. Built exclusively to house the museum's medieval art collection, this extension of the Met is almost too gothic. Haunting Gregorian chant fills the air; visitors shuffle past through shadowy, vaulted passage-ways … I felt an urge to don monk's robes and shave my head.

The utter serenity of this hilltop monastery is always inspiring. Purchased in 1925 by the Met with a donation by John D. Rockefeller Jr., The Cloisters was opened as a branch of the museum in 1938. Rockefeller purchased a tract of land across the river to preserve its arcadian views, then shipped original architectural elements from five cloisters in France to be reconstructed as the centerpieces of this medieval world high above the Hudson. Everything here is authentic — from the magnificent Unicorn tapestries and Romanesque colonnades to the cobblestone courtyards and curative herb garden.

So if you're a fan of time travel, just board the A train for thirteenth-century Europe and experience this evocative, mysterious medieval world.

P.S. The gargoyles are harmless.

Conservatory Garden

Address: 105th St. and Fifth Ave.
Hours: Daily; 8 A.M. to Dusk
Admission: Free
Subway: 6 to 103rd St., walk west
Bus: M1, 2, 3, 4 (Fifth or Madison Aves.) to
105th St.

In the first edition of this book, I revealed the special joys of the Conservatory Garden, and yet it remains the best-kept secret in Manhattan. New York's only formal garden stands elegantly at 105th Street and Fifth Avenue across from the Museum of the City of New York. This is uncharted territory for many residents and visitors who haven't yet discovered the city's attractions above 96th Street. What are you waiting for?

The six-acre garden is a perfectly safe place to visit, in addition to being one of the few official "Quiet Zones" in this city that actually is. Whenever I enter the huge wrought iron gates, I immediately feel that I've stepped into the sweeping backyard of a stately English home. There are precisely trimmed hedges, enchanting arbors, ornate flower beds, sculpted fountains, and one of the most spectacular pergolas you will ever see — all perfectly styled in the Victorian tradition.

The south end, also called The Secret Garden as a tribute to the Frances Hodgson Burnett children's classic, seems always to be filled with endless birdsong. It has particular charm with its whimsical fountain, hidden niches, and bountiful flower beds.

Traveler's Note: Five blocks north through the park, The Central Park Conservancy has transformed the Harlem Meer (Dutch for "lake") from a swampy soup of algae and detritus into pristine wetlands and a sandy beach. The Dana Discovery Center, at shore's edge, offers a rich program of hands-on science projects and fishing for city kids. It's all free.

Dia
Center Rooftop

**Address: 548 W. 22nd St. bet. Tenth and
Eleventh Aves.**
Phone: 989-5566
**Hours: Wednesday through Sunday, Noon to
6 P.M., closed July and August**
**Admission: $6 suggested donation; $3 seniors
and students**
Subway: A, C, E to 23rd St., walk W.
Bus: M11 (Tenth Ave.) to 23rd St.
Web site: www.diacenter.org

there is something about being on a rooftop in New York that evokes feelings of magic and romance.

Perhaps it's those unforgettable silver-screen images of Marlon Brando in *On The Waterfront* with his loft-loving pigeons, or *West Side Story*'s moon-lit love scenes between Tony and Maria. Whatever it is, I do know that standing high above the city with nothing but a cloudless sky above is infinitely liberating. They know it at Dia Center for the Arts, too.

Dia is a 35,000-square-foot facility that presents the work of emerging contemporary artists in full-floor, long-term exhibitions. This unusual arrangement allows visitors to ponder art in an open, unconfined setting.

Dia's one permanent installation is an interactive piece by artist Dan Graham — an intriguing glass and metal configuration for the rooftop that is, in itself, a "reflective" experience. A small, room-sized glass box surrounds a smaller cylinder of 2-way mirror. When the observer steps into the sculpture (participation is intended) it becomes a multisensory adventure. An adjacent café and video salon provides alfresco rest and sustenance.

While the Dia Center rooftop may not sit on the city's tallest building, it does offer a remote roosting place for safety and solitude above the teeming streets.

Equitable Tower Atrium

Address: 787 Seventh Ave. between 51st and
52nd Sts.
Hours: Daily, 10 A.M. to 6 P.M.
Admission: Free
Subway: N, R to 49th St.; 1 or 9 to 50th St.
Bus: M6, 7 (Seventh Ave.) to 51st St.

Some years back the city began offering generous financial incentives to builders who provided public atriums, plazas and open spaces. They responded with a contrasting mix of macabre, mall-like settings and truly magnificent retreats.

One of the best is the Equitable Atrium, where they've tucked away a gift of solitude: a forty-foot, semicircular marble settee. This curving bench is a sculptural, spatial and acoustical phenomenon. I will never understand how it works, but take just a few steps inside this sky-lit crescent and you have the distinct sensation of being held firmly in a protective marble cocoon. Add the flora-filled marble fountain and dense screen of tropical conifers, and it becomes nearly impossible to leave this gentle embrace.

Roy Lichenstein's "Mural with Blue Brushstroke" dominates the wall behind this benevolent bench enclosure. Painted on site in 1984, it is a monumental piece by the celebrated Pop artist.

Here are other public spaces I rate highly: Crystal Pavillion (Third Avenue and 50th Street): The stainless steel decor is a tad cold, but two shimmering water walls on the lower level warm things up. Continental Atrium (Maiden Lane and Front Street): The intricate Tinker Toy interior is a playful place to relax. J.P.Morgan Building (60 Wall Street): With a trickling fountain and ample seating the galleria is a receptive retreat for perusing the *Wall Street Journal.*

Erol Beker
Chapel
of St. Peter's Church

Address: Lexington Ave. at 54th St.
Phone: 935-2200
Hours: Daily, 8 A.M. to 8 P.M.
Admission: Free
Subway: 6 to 51st St.
Bus: M101, M102 (Lexington and Third Aves.)
to 51st St.

What if you owned a tiny parcel of land in the center of Manhattan, and you had an insatiable desire for peace and quiet? And what if you decided to transform that sliver of land into a private corner of celestial calm, a hushed and happy place with interior design by acclaimed American sculptor Louise Nevelson?

Well, I'm guessing it would look and feel a whole lot like the inviolate surroundings of the Erol Beker Chapel — as much an exuberant work of modern art as a dulcet haven for heart and soul.

This is Nevelson's only permanent sculptural environment in New York City, and she wanted the unique prayer space, tucked inside the north wall of St. Peter's Church (the jagged appendage at the base of the Citicorp complex), to "exude purity." That's why everything in this twenty-eight by twenty-one foot, five-sided chapel is white: white painted sculptural elements on white walls; white floors; white altar; and white pews. Even its one window is frosted white.

I am unable to pass within five blocks of this thumb-sized peace pocket without its enthralling gravity drawing me in. The stillness here is palpable. Just gaze into the solitary sanctuary lamp for a minute and you'll return to the streets a more agreeable human being.

The Flower Garden at W. 91st Street

Address: Riverside Park at 91st St.
Hours: Daily, 24 Hours
Admission: Free
Subway: 1, 9 to 86th St., walk northwest
Bus: M5 (Riverside Drive) to 91st St.

When Upper Westsiders mention "our garden," they're often referring to the flower garden at 91st Street in Riverside Park.

While not a community garden per se, its planting and upkeep are entrusted to local residents. The fenced flower beds —about one-hundred yards west of Riverside Drive — have a beauty and grandeur that seems to quiet minds and mouths. Sit along the benches surrounding the garden and you'll notice that conversations are muted, apparently hushed out of respect for the blooming orchestra of natural splendor.

The garden is a fragrant cul-de-sac set within a grove of crabapple and dogwood trees that bloom luxuriously in the spring; and it is also the turnaround point for a broad esplanade favored by joggers and bikers.

The esplanade, with its elevated views of the Hudson River, is divided by a wide grass median that extends to 83rd Street. I treasure photographs of my father walking along this exact stretch of Riverside Park in the 1940s, proving perhaps that the desire to find peace and quiet in New York is a genetic predisposition.

Traveler's Note: One-hundred-fifty feet above the garden and two blocks south is the Soldiers and Sailors Monument, another wonderful spot for peaceful repose. This huge circular monument has massive marble and concrete terraces overlooking Riverside Park and New Jersey, with broad stone benches on which to, literally, cool your heels.

Ford Foundation Building

Address: 320 East 43rd St. between First and
Second Aves.
Phone: 573-5000
Hours: Monday through Friday,
9 A.M. to 5 P.M.
Admission: Free
Subway: 4, 5, 6 to Grand Central, walk east
Bus: M15 (First and Second Aves.) to 42nd St.;
M104 or M42 crosstown to Second Ave.

In a stroke of architectural genius, the designer of the Ford Foundation — Kevin Roche — placed the building around the park, instead of the other way around. Here you can enjoy a 160-foot high, glass-walled, third-of-an-acre terraced garden, lushly landscaped with exotic greenery.

Because there are no benches or chairs, and no food or drinks allowed, Roche's towering green-house plaza does not draw the crowds other public spaces seem to attract. In fact, the rainforest-like setting is almost always unoccupied.

You'll be most comfortable ascending to the east side of the top tier, where you'll find a three-foot, sun-drenched sitting wall, a quiet vantage point from which to study the seventeen full-grown trees (including acacia, magnolia, and eucalyptus), 1000 shrubs, 150 vines, and 21,900 ground cover plants. The landscapers also rotate special plantings for each season with tulips in spring, begonias in summer, chrysanthemums in fall and poinsettias in winter. The three levels of garden court are lined with brick pathways descending to a still-water pool, which gratefully accepts your coins on behalf of UNICEF (appropriate, with the United Nations located just half a block east).

At the Ford Foundation the air is dense with the earthy scent of bursting horticulture, a kind of intoxicating chlorophyll panacea guaranteed to calm the most hyperactive minds.

The Frick Collection

Address: 1 East 70th St. at Fifth Ave.
Phone: 288-0700
Hours: Tuesday through Saturday,
10 A.M. to 6 P.M.;
Sunday, 1 to 6 P.M.; closed Monday
Admission: $7
Subway: 6 to 68th St., walk west
Bus: M1, 2, 3, 4 (Fifth and Madison Aves.)
to 68th St.

i think it's the frogs that make the Frick.

That might sound odd until you visit the former

mansion of Henry Clay Frick, now the home of

one of New York's most illustrious art collec-

tions. Enter on 70th Street and walk directly

back to the sky-lit Garden Court. That's where

you'll see the two frisky frogs, perpetually spout-

ing water at each other from either end of a long

fountain. This water play is mesmerizing, and the

planted Garden Court, with its polished floors

and marble benches, is immeasurably soothing.

The Frick's residential setting and unhurried ambience are ideal for viewing the formidable art collection, including some of the best known European paintings by celebrated artists such as Velazquez, Van Dyck, Vermeer, El Greco, and Goya. Most of the museum's rooms are lit by skylights, including the West Gallery where I defy any mortal man or woman to sit on the ample sofas facing one of Rembrandt's striking self-portraits and not feel overcome by the sublime beauty.

One minor rub: Like me, you'll probably ache to get out on the west portico and elegant outdoor terraces. Unfortunately, they're inexplicably (and forever) closed to the public.

You'll have to settle for the art ... and the frogs.

The General
Theological
Seminary

**Address: 175 Ninth Ave. between 20th and
21st St.**
Phone: 243-5150
**Hours: Monday through Friday, Noon to 3 P.M.;
Saturday 11 A.M. to 3 P.M.; Closed Sunday**
Admission: Free
Subway: A, C, E to 23rd St.; 1 to 18th St.
Bus: M11 (Ninth and Tenth Aves.) to 23rd St.

Combine the pastoral serenity of a New England campus quad with the cloistered formality of an English collegiate close, and you'll appreciate the little hint of heaven they've created at the seminary of the Episcopal Church in Chelsea.

When I first entered the pristine grounds (you must sign in at the Ninth Ave. entrance), I was utterly amazed that this space was available to me — it really is that special. But the seminarians here are extraordinarily friendly people who want to contribute to their community, and have generously done so with this outdoor "peace offering." They'll even respond to a visitor's naive questions about the seminary's exquisite architecture with a polite and patient smile … (it's nineteenth-century Gothic Revival).

The red brick buildings which frame the seminary grounds were built beginning in 1836 and cover an entire city block. The complex is also a registered National Historic Landmark. Don't miss the Chapel of the Good Shepherd at the heart of the block-long quad. It's a charming, simple, country-like chapel that glows with the warmth of beautiful stained glass and dark, rich wood carvings. After strolling the landscaped pathways of the seminary's outer yard, I've always found the chapel an ideal place to explore my own inner pathways.

Greenacre Park

Address: 221 East 51st St. between Second and Third Aves.
Hours: Daily, 8 A.M. to 6 P.M.
Admission: Free
Subway: E or F to 53rd St.;
6 to 51st St., walk east
Bus: M101 (Lexington and Third Aves.) to 51st St.

this vest-pocket park in the heart of the East Midtown commercial and residential district is nowhere near an acre, but it does offer an acre's worth of rare tranquility.

Like Paley Park, its smaller cousin a few blocks away on East 53rd Street, Greenacre Park boasts a dramatic two-story waterfall, this one constructed of massive granite blocks. There's a babbling brook here, too, which ambles along the east wall and empties into a plunge pool. The intermingling sounds of gurgling, flowing, and cascading water significantly mask street noise, insulating this very pleasant park from the incessant tug of the city.

I particularly recommend the park on rainy days when you can ponder the waterfalls alone, undisturbed, and comfortably dry under the trellis roof of the west terrace, where you'll find plenty of outdoor chairs and tables. In good weather, however, Greenacre Park is no place to linger during weekday lunch hours when local business people swarm here to soak in the sun and quiet.

The park brochure says it was designed "to provide a place for the general public to gain special repose from the increasing city experience of noise, concrete, and humdrum." Makes me feel like humming just thinking about it.

Green-Wood Cemetery

Address: Fifth Ave. at 25th St., Brooklyn
Phone: (718) 768-7300
Hours: Daily, 8 A.M. to 4 P.M.
Admission: Free
Subway: N, R to 25th St., walk east
Auto: Brooklyn Battery Tunnel onto the
Brooklyn Queens Expressway (BQE), to Third
Ave. exit, left on 25th St. to Fifth Ave.

forget for a moment that there are 500,000 dead people here.

Consider instead that this rural cemetery was designed in 1838 by civil engineer David Bates Douglass as a pastoral park with rolling hills, five lakes, thirty miles of serpentine pathways, and some of the city's oldest trees — all in a bucolic setting half the size of Central Park.

Within this sepulchral masterpiece situated at the highest point in Brooklyn, you'll find no cars, no trucks, no subways, no sirens, no screaming kids

— and virtually no (living) people. The stillness here is profound, a lot like what you'd find at, well, a cemetery.

Green-Wood has the additional appeal of its celebrity occupants, among whom are stained-glass master Louis Comfort Tiffany, pencil man Eberhard Faber, piano maker Henry Steinway, and soap magnate William Colgate. And I discovered recently why Green-Wood Cemetery has a particularly magical air. This is the eternal resting place of actor Frank Morgan. You know...The Wizard of Oz.

Traveler's Note: A walking tour of the famous monuments by ex-policeman and Green-Wood buff John Cashman is conducted on Sundays in the spring and fall for a nominal fee. Call ahead for times and gathering location.

Inwood Hill Park

Address: 207th St. and Seaman Ave.
Hours: Daily, Dawn to dusk
Admission: Free
Subway: A, 1, 9 to 207th St.
Bus: M100 (Amsterdam Ave.) to 207th St.

m y childhood home bordered a large, wooded nature preserve. From my bedroom window, I viewed this seemingly endless forest as a dark, dangerous place. But as I grew older, it became a friend; a private world to wander in, to be alone in, to conjure grand visions in, or to cry, openly and unobserved.

I have been able to reconnect with that secret forest of my childhood at Inwood Hill Park. This beautiful, rustic, rocky park is the largest expanse of natural woodland left in Manhattan. You can walk along miles of meandering pathways within its 196-acre wilderness, or blaze your own trails over mossy glens, fallen trees, and sparse underbrush. Flag down one of the patrolling Urban Park Rangers to secure a useful, hand-drawn trail map. Inwood Park holds two special surprises: the mysterious Indian Caves which remain largely undisturbed (you'll find them at the park's center, near Pothole Road on the map), and Manhattans' only sizable salt marsh in the valley section of the park. Visit this brackish habitat to spy herons, egrets, hawks, and an occasional raccoon fishing for oysters.

Historians will note the marked boulder where it is believed Peter Minuit bought Manhattan Island from the Reckgawawanc Indians for trinkets worth about 60 Dutch guilders. Proves what I often say — you just can't stretch a guilder the way you used to.

Traveler's Note: Look for the spectacular cliff outcroppings overlooking the Hudson River at the western edge of the park. You can usually shimmy through a rolled-back fence opening to the most scenic picnicking spot in the city.

Isamu Noguchi
Garden Museum

Address: 32-37 Vernon Blvd., Long Island City, Queens
Phone: (718) 204-7088
Hours: Wednesday, Thursday, Friday, 10 A.M. to 5 P.M., Saturday, Sunday 11 A.M. to 6 P.M., April through November
Admission: $4 suggested donation
Subway: N to Broadway (Long Island City), walk west nine blocks to Vernon Blvd, south two blocks to museum
Shuttle Bus: call for information
Construction Note: Until Spring 2004, the museum will be undergoing renovation and will be operating from a temporary location. Call for information.

Isamu Noguchi, the late Japanese-American sculptor, would sometimes study a piece of raw marble or granite for years before making the first strike. He called this process "discovering the stone's essence."

At the Isamu Noguchi Garden Museum, I can almost feel the master artist urging me to take up my own, inner sculpting tools — to split and cut, chisel and polish — to discover the essence of self. Noguchi's sculptures always speak this personally and deeply.

This dignified, uncluttered, unexpectedly tranquil gallery and garden is situated in the heart of Long Island City's industrial waterfront, where Noguchi could be close to the marble cutting shops in the area. The museum contains more than 250 Noguchi sculptures of stone, wood and clay, as well as his mulberry-bark-paper and bamboo Akari light sculptures. Each is placed with precision and sensitivity to elicit the most profound reaction. The peacefulness of the sculpture garden alone, enjoyed year round by a family of doves, rewards the extra effort it takes to get here. I suggest a day trip, so you'll have time to absorb the illuminating messages Noguchi has chiseled into his oracular boulders.

Traveler's Note: While you're here, make a point to walk two blocks north to Socrates Park, an awe-inspiring, riverfront creation that's home to outdoor sculpture on a towering scale. You'll see.

The Jacqueline Onassis Reservoir Running Path

Address: Mid Central Park, 86th to 96th Sts.
Hours: Daily, 24 hours
Admission: Free
Subway: 4, 5, 6 to 86th St., walk west to entrance at 89th St. and Fifth Ave.
Bus: M1, 2, 3, 4 to 86th St.

You've certainly heard of "runner's high" — that state of quasi-euphoria every serious aerobic athlete experiences. In New York, we have our own unique version called "reservoir runner's high." It kicks in with sweet reliability after a lap or two around the spectacular reservoir path.

A big body of water like this one attracts a large variety of migrating water fowl, along with the normal contingent of local mallards and seagulls. A bridle path runs parallel to the track for much of its length, so it's not unusual to find yourself matching strides with an equestrian or two. The combined effect makes a circuit of the elevated, 1.6-mile cinder path the equivalent of jogging the perimeter of a country lake.

You'll encounter other striders along the way, but these are conscientious, quiet athletes. It's a very civilized group. And if you stand by the South Gate House (86th Street, looking due north), you'll see one of my favorite sights in Manhattan — a building-less horizon. You can cast your gaze far out into the distance from here and behold only water, trees, and flocks of birds. What a relief for your skyscraped eyes.

The picturesque reservoir path is more than a spot for furtive celebrity watching; it's a refreshing island of water in a big stone sea.

Drink deeply.

Jacques Marchais
Center of Tibetan Art

Address: 338 Lighthouse Ave., Staten Island
Phone: (718) 351-0402
Hours: April to November, Wednesday through
Sunday, 1 to 5 P.M.
November to March, Wednesday through
Friday, 1 to 5 P.M.
Admission: $5 adults, $2 children
Bus: From Staten Island Ferry, take S74 to
Lighthouse Ave., then ten minute walk up hill
(allow ninety minutes total from Manhattan)
Auto: Call for directions
Web site: www.tibetanmuseum.com

this cliff-clinging museum on Staten Island incorporates a recreation of a Tibetan monastery temple that is so authentic, Buddhist monks frequently come here to perform rituals and practices.

The creation of Jacqueline Klauber, who used the name Jacques Marchais for professional reasons, the museum holds one of the largest collections of Tibetan art outside of Tibet. The lamasery altar is so jam-packed with gilded Buddhas, ornate prayer wheels, elaborate incense burners, and startling ritual masks, you'll wonder how peaceful prayer ever happens here...until you let the transformative powers of these sacred objects envelope you.

Located at the highest point on the eastern seaboard, the center doesn't exactly have Himalayan vistas, but its distant harbor views are venerated locally. On the tranquil patio garden you'll also see huge baboons, trumpeting elephants, and prancing rabbits...all of the stone variety. The goldfish in the lotus pond, however, are real.

See those colorful prayer flags fluttering in the trees? It is believed that the wind carries their blessings and messages out to the world. So I prayed for more places just like this one.

Traveler's Note: The Center has an extensive calendar of Far Eastern related events. Call for a list.

John Finley Walk at Carl Schurz Park

Address: 84th to 89th St. and East End. Ave.
Hours: Daily, dawn to 1 A.M.
Admission: Free
Subway: 4, 5, 6 to 86th St.
Bus: M86 (86th St. crosstown) to York Ave.,
walk east.; M31 (York Ave.) to 86th St.

Carl Schurz Park is one of those places in the city you know you've heard of but can't quite pinpoint.

Apparently a lot of city residents and visitors have trouble finding this place, so it remains a bona fide refuge for peace-and-quiet seekers and strollers. To access this smallish (10.3 acre) neighborhood park and the John Finley Walk, climb the broad circular stairs at the 86th Street entrance until you reach the elevated promenade. Once there, you can amble along past Gracie Mansion absorbing the history of the century-old, panoramic, and unusually safe park

(Hizzoner's house is on the property, so it's well guarded). This is a park for young families and elderly people who gather to enjoy sweeping views of the East River and Roosevelt Island. It's breathtaking at night when river bridges are brightly lit, throwing luminous reflections off the water.

There's a children's playground at the south end that can be noisy. For optimum privacy, walk north along the promenade past the flagpole to where the footpath narrows. Continue for another 100 feet (if you reach the fireboat house you've gone too far) and settle yourself down on a shaded bench. You'll know when you've reached the right place by that telltale sound — the sound of silence.

Kayaking at the Downtown Boathouse

Address: Downtown Boathouse, Pier 26 on the Hudson River, between Hubert and North Moore Sts.
Phone: 385-2790
Hours: 9 A.M. to 6 P.M., Saturdays, Sundays, and Holidays, mid-May through mid-October
Admission: Free
Subway: 1, 9 to Franklin St., walk west
Bus: M10 (Eighth Ave.) to North Moore St., walk west

for avid kayakers, the Hudson River is considered "Big Water" — powerful, demanding, deserving of respect. But despite the tricky currents, strong winds and floating detritus, it is possible to experience this tidal river safely, peacefully, and with profound, eye-level intimacy in a kayak.

By law the city has to provide public access to navigable waters from designated piers and boat launches. In this case, they've authorized the volunteer, not-for-profit Downtown Boathouse to offer education and easy access for canoeists and kayakers. And, incredibly, it's all free — use of the kayaks, basic instruction, your time on the water.

Under the responsible, safety-first tutelage of these dedicated volunteers, you're given a life-vest, oar, and kayak, and sent off to explore the relatively protected waters of the adjacent embay-ment. The public kayaks, virtually roll-proof and excellent for beginners, are called "sit-on-tops" because they have no cockpit.

Once you're bobbing on the water — just body, boat and blade — you experience what addicted "river rats" describe as a transcendent union with your surroundings: expansive water, open sky, the light slapping of ripples against the boat, the swish of your oar. You see the busyness and the bustle on shore, but you are not there. You are not in the city at all. You are here, dipped into liquid nature.

If kayaking gets your full attention, and it can, contact the New York Kayak Company (924-1327/www.nykayak.com) for expert instruction and all-day sea kayaking adventures.

La Casa Day Spa
Floatation

Address: 41 East 20th St. bet. Park Ave. and Broadway
Phone: 673-2272
Hours: Monday and Tuesday, 12 P.M. to 6 P.M.;
Wednesday to Friday, 10 A.M. to 8 P.M.;
Saturday and Sunday, 10 A.M. to 6 P.M.
Admission: $50 for one hour float/
$25 if combined with one hour of bodywork (separate fee)
Subway: 4, 5, 6 to 23rd St.
Bus: M101 (Park Ave., uptown, and Third Ave., downtown) to 20th St.
Web site: www.lacasaspa.com

You're naked. Your body is completely relaxed. You're floating weightlessly in your own private sea, a warm, silky liquid rocking you into a state of suspended tranquility.

It's probably safe to say that the last time you experienced this level of bliss was at the threshold of your current incarnation — in the womb. Unless, perhaps, you're a habitual "floater". At this floatation center and day spa (massage, facials, and wraps), they maintain a state-of-the-art floatation room with adjoining private shower. All you bring is your overtaxed body. Begin by decompressing in La Casa's tastefully appointed "tropical" reception area, then get ready to climb into ten inches of water so thoroughly infused with epsom salts, anything (and anyone) will float.

By adjusting light and music levels, you control the degree of sensory deprivation; the fewer external stimuli, the better. Within seconds your buoyant body releases into the anti-gravity effects and the mind voyage begins.

In this liquid cocoon you'll experience all things good, from profound relaxation to genuine euphoria. Studies even suggest that a two-hour float can be more restful than a full night's sleep. Which all adds up to the kind of out-of-body sensation you'll want to dive right into.

Lady Mendl's Tea Salon

Address: 56 Irving Pl. at 17th St.
Phone: 533-4466
Hours: Wednesday through Friday, 3 P.M. seating; Saturday and Sunday,
2 P.M. or 4:30 P.M. seatings
Admission: $30.00 per person, reservations required
Subway: 4,5, 6 to 14th St., walk east
Bus: M1, 2, 3, 4 (Fifth Ave.), walk east
Web site: www.innatirving.com

If everyone in New York were required to break for afternoon tea, I'm sure we'd all feel a bit more civilized and a lot less harried.

I've sampled tea time at various places around town in search of the serenity and sophistication associated with this rite, and I think it's done with unusual charm and elegance in the nostalgic parlor of Lady Mendl's Tea Salon. Situated in a lovingly restored 1834 townhouse in Gramercy Park, the salon is tastefully decorated with uphol-stered arm chairs and antiques of the era, including period china and silver tea services. The mellow mood is heightened by the flickering flames from a pair of cozy fireplaces.

The delectable, five-course afternoon tea includes fresh fruit, finger sandwiches, sweet scones with jam, macaroons, and a final sublime pastry offering. More than 20 fine aromatic teas are available, but you will do well to choose the smoky Formosa Oolong or Fancy Ceylon. After an hour and a half of tea and easy conversation at Lady Mendl's, a guest and I concluded our genteel visit to the last century with a stroll around the historic Gramercy Park neighborhood.

While several midtown hotels also serve afternoon tea, I like the informality of two other downtown locations: Tsalon & Temporium (11 East 20th Street, 358-0506) for its casual geniality, and Anglers and Writers (420 Hudson Street, 675-0810) where you can sip Earl Grey under the watchful eyes of several wall-mounted trout.

Lighthouse
Park on
Roosevelt Island

Address: Northern tip of Roosevelt Island
Phone: 832-4543
Hours: Daily, 24 hours
Admission: Free
Subway: B, Q to Roosevelt Island
Tram: Departs from 59th St. and Second Ave.

there's nothing like escaping to a quiet island

when the city encroaches on your sanity.

Especially when this quiet island is only five min-

utes away.

I wonder why so few New Yorkers think of

Roosevelt Island as a viable getaway? Do they

worry they'll get over there and never find their

way back? Or that the aerial tram will deposit

them in the river before it lands them safely on

the opposite shore (you can also take a subway)?

Let me dispel all fears: Not only can you get to

tranquil Lighthouse Park quickly and safely, you

can also buy a sandwich at an island deli, catch a half hour of unobstructed rays, and be back at the office before anyone notices.

The short tram ride ($1.50 each way) is an event in itself. You can see virtually every inch of Manhattan (most of Queens, too) from 250 feet up on the soaring Swiss cable cars. Once on this sliver of land, take the red bus (fare is 25 cents) as far north as it travels, then stroll along the island's east side until you reach the park. You'll probably see a few fishermen near the tiny granite lighthouse and not much else. You'll also find a wide lawn, hospitable picnic tables, and an exercise course for those inclined.

For loafers like me, the extent of island activity involves reclining on a grassy ridge counting barges as they glide by.

The Lotus Garden

Address: 97th St. bet. Broadway and
West End Ave.
Phone: 580-4897
Hours: April to mid-November, Sundays,
1 P.M. to 4 P.M. to the public; Daily,
dawn to dusk for key-holders
Admission: Free on Sundays
Subway: 1, 9 to 96th St.
Bus: M104 to 96th St.

there are few things more astonishing in this city than to witness nature assert itself in unlikely places — a dandelion rising from a mound of silt and dust on a rooftop, an oak sapling poking out from a crack in the sidewalk.

No clearer evidence of nature's reassuring determination exists than at the remarkable little Lotus Garden, sitting 20 feet above 97th Street atop a busy garage. Working with local developers in 1983, activists Mark Greenwald, an architect, and Carrie Maher, a horticulturist, spearheaded the garden's design with other neighbors.

Creating this riot of fragrant color over a garage rooftop involved spreading three-and-a-half feet of topsoil over the entire 7,000-square-foot-expanse.

There are no actual lotus plants in the garden, but you'll find abundant water lilies thriving in two small goldfish ponds. The garden is artfully subdivided into member-tended plots from which grow peach, apple, and cherry trees, fragrant herbs, and bountiful blooms for all seasons.

Open to the public only on Sundays, you can purchase a key granting you lifetime entrance to this elevated oasis for only $15. During my first visit to this unique shade garden, I strolled the wood-chip lined pathways, I wrote, I sniffed the blossoms in a dozen flower beds, then sat quietly alone, journeying to the deepest part of my being. Twenty minutes later, I became a key-holder to this little-known treasure forever.

Mount Vernon Hotel
Museum & Garden

Address: 421 East 61st St. between First and
York Aves.
Phone: 838-6878
Hours: Tuesday through Sunday, 11 A.M. to
4 P.M.; closed Monday
Admission: $4
Subway: 4, 5, 6 to 59th St., walk east
Bus: M15 (First and Second Aves.); M57
(57th St. crosstown) to First Ave., walk north

When you walk through the gates of this charming museum, you enter more than a peaceful enclave — you pass into another era.

Constructed in 1799, this former carriage house is one of only seven surviving eighteenth-century buildings in Manhattan still open to the public. In 1826 it was converted to the fashionable Mount Vernon Hotel catering to affluent New Yorkers who would escape to the "country" from the southern tip of Manhattan. Guests would leave the crowded city for this "day hotel," where they could enjoy rural walks, horse racing, fishing, salt water bathing, and other country pastimes in what is now midtown. Mount Vernon is the only former day hotel still standing in the city.

After decades of neglect during the late 1800s, the handsome stone hotel was purchased and restored by The Colonial Dames of America in 1924, who filled the museum's nine rooms with furniture and artifacts of the Federal period. The museum tour is well worth taking; however, I was most attracted to the reconstructed eighteenth-century garden. Once you pay for the tour, the kindly docents will let you sit in the backyard garden all day among the precisely planted flora and colorful perennials.

In the northwest corner of the garden, steps lead to a particularly peaceful upper terrace, where there's a natural schist outcropping (the same Manhattan stone quarried to build the museum) ideal for spring and summer sunning. The garden is transformed into a place for tea parties and concerts Tuesday evenings in June and July.

The New York Botanical Garden

Address: 200th St. at Southern Blvd., Bronx
Phone: (718) 817-8700
Hours: Tuesday through Sunday, 10 A.M. to 6
P.M. (4 P.M. Winter) Admission: $1.50 for
grounds only; $7.50 for all attractions;
parking $5
Train: Metro North (Harlem Line) from Grand
Central to Botanical Garden stop
Auto: Henry Hudson Pkwy. to Exit 24, Moshulu
Pkwy. to Botanical Garden exit, turn right on
Southern Blvd., to gardens

Your sense of smell is the most acute sense
you have, a fact that makes a trip to the
New York Botanical Garden one of the most
sensual experiences there is.

With 250 quiet acres of blooming, burgeoning,
bursting gardens, plus the spectacular turn-of-
the-century Haupt conservatory, this is an all-
season olfactory feast. The clever horticulturists
here have carefully planned a succession of flowers and foliage that keep the grounds in almost
full color and fragrance from spring's first thaw

to the onset of winter. Scent engulfs you — sweet
and spicy, pungent and bitter. The air, laden with
nature's infinite perfumes, is a pleasure
to breathe.

Let your nose lead you to the heady, organic
smells of the last uncut forest in the city — forty
acres of hemlock, oak, maple and hickory (some
trees more than two hundred fifty years old)
crisscrossed with mulch-covered trails. There's a
serene conifer forest, too; giant evergreens towering above an aromatic bed of balsamic pine nee-
dles — perhaps life's most wistful essence.

There are so many pleasurable scents emanating
from the Botanical Garden, you'll want to arrive
early and leave late. It's the only way to fully
inhale New York's most ambrosial experience.

The
New York
Earth Room

**Address: 141 Wooster St. (half-block south of
Houston St.)
Phone: 473-8072
Hours: Wednesday through Saturday, Noon to
6 P.M.; closed June to September
Admission: Free
Subway: N or R to Prince St., walk west
Bus: M1, 6 (Broadway) to Prince St.**

here's the dirt: One of New York's most pristine yet peculiar sanctuaries is a SoHo loft filled with 280,000 pounds of topsoil.

The Earth Room is the creation of artist Walter De Maria, a taciturn man who has little to say about his humble earth sculpture. Nevertheless, this inert, silent scene makes its own powerful statement about city life — or more correctly, about the absence of pastoral simplicity in our lives.

After the predictable exclamations of disbelief, you'll sink into the disarming vibrations of this austere space, "empty" except for the 3,600 square feet of wall-to-wall soil and a few mushrooms. Hunker down behind the low Plexiglas partition so that the huge expanse of earth is at eye level. Breathe in the sweet smell and cool moisture-laden air emanating from the rich black loam. Plunge your hands into the soil — it's allowed. Let the good earth remind you that it always lies softly underfoot, a healing cushion too easily forgotten in a city where an impenetrable concrete crust separates you from Nature's own terra firma below.

Apart from a few regulars who revive themselves weekly at this friendly, fallow field, you can call the Earth Room your own. Just don't pick the mushrooms.

New York Public Library and Bryant Park

Address: 42nd St. bet. Fifth to Sixth Aves.
Phone: 869-8089
Hours: Library open Monday, Thursday, Friday,
Saturday 10 A.M. to 6 P.M.; Tuesday and
Wednesday, 11 A.M. to 7:30 P.M.
Park open daily 8 A.M. to Dusk
Admission: Free
Subway: 4, 5, 6 to Grand Central, walk west
Bus: M1, 2, 3, 4 (Fifth and Madison Aves.)
to 42nd St.; M42 (42nd St. crosstown)
to Fifth Ave.
Web site: www.nypl.org

What's so special about a public library?

Well, this is not just any library, it's New York's Big Library. And it happens to have a lush green carpet running the length of its backyard. So whether you go to see the lions, Patience and Fortitude, who guard the front entrance, or the imposing architecture, or the splendid exhibits, you'll be treated to plenty of peace and quiet here.

While the vast main reading room on the third

floor (room 315) is relatively noise-free, even greater seclusion exists just down the hall in room 313, Art and Architecture. Provided you're there to use the collection, no one will bother you. If you can finagle a pass to one of the private study rooms, such as room 320, the Berg Collection, you'll find ancient volumes on arcane subjects, and absolute silence.

Once you feel properly edified inside, go out back to the library's six-acre masterpiece of a makeover; Bryant Park, designed by Lynden B. Miller, was transformed in the mid-nineties from a spooky tangle of hedges infested with drug dealers into a sweet, secure, superbly-conceived city park. The thick-growing lawn, lovingly maintained perimeter gardens, and spindly metal lawn chairs — all reminiscent of Paris' famed Luxembourg Gardens — facilitate hours of mind-less rest and relaxation.

Nicholas Roerich Museum

Address: 319 West 107th St. bet. Broadway
and Riverside Dr.
Phone: 864-7752
Hours: Tuesday through Sunday, 2 to 5 P.M.
Admission: Free
Subway: 1, 9 to 110th St, walk south
Bus: M5, M104 to 107th St.

a trek through the Himalayan foothills is often characterized as the ultimate spiritual journey — as close as you can get to God and heaven with your feet still on the ground. If neither your schedule nor your budget permit a Himalayan expedition anytime soon, a vicarious trek through the nearby Nicholas Roerich Museum might prove a worthy substitute.

This little known treasury contains more than 200 paintings by the Russian-born Roerich (1874-1947), a mystic, artist and author who lived in the Himalayas for much of his life. Respected internationally for his efforts to promote peace through culture, Roerich was also nominated for the Nobel Peace Prize in 1929. The casual town house dedicated to his work and spirit is furnished parlor style to encourage leisurely, deliberate viewing of his expansive mountain scenes.

Allow Roerich's luminous landscape paintings — vibrant with tempera blues, whites, violets, and reds — to lift you up and carry you on a cloud of color to the roof of the world.

There is not a disappointing painting on the entire three floors of this blissful brownstone, but if you really want your soul to fly, go directly to Kanchenjunga (front room, second floor). This magnificent image of a Himalayan peak will send you to another realm.

Open Center
Meditation Room

**Address: 83 Spring St. bet. Broadway
and Crosby St.
Phone: 219-2527
Hours: Daily, 10 A.M. to 10 P.M.
Admission: Free
Subway: N or R to Prince St.; 6 to Spring St.
Bus: M1, 6 (Broadway) to Spring St.
Web site: www.opencenter.org**

he Open Center is the largest urban holistic center in the world, offering hundreds of fascinating courses for exploring consciousness, creativity and spirit. The Center describes itself as a "space into which we can withdraw from routine preoccupations," and people of all ages have found a supportive and healing environment here.

While the Center holds many soul-sustaining attractions, my favorite is on the second floor where you'll find a room dedicated exclusively to private meditation. The incense-laden peace of this space has been enhanced by a blessing from an esteemed Tibetan lama. Also take note of the mottled rose and lilac-colored walls, the work of architectural painter, John Stolfo, who was commissioned by the Center to apply his "Lazure" painting technique (based on the teachings of Rudolf Steiner) to the room. Using natural-pigment, non-toxic paints combined with essential healing oils, Stolfo created rhythmic patterns on the walls intended to help meditators achieve a deeper contemplative experience. I've serenity-sampled the room both before and after the mood-altering paint job and was impressed by the subtle difference.

The Open Center's meditation room offers a comforting place to pause during the day for a moment's reflection. And be sure to stop by the bookstore where you'll find a unique collection of holistic and spiritual books, New Age CDs, and accessories for your home altar.

Paley Park

**Address: 53rd St. between Fifth and Madison
Aves.
Hours: Monday through Saturday, 8 A.M. to
7:45 P.M.
Admission: Free
Subway: E or F to Fifth Ave/53rd St.
Bus: M1, 2, 3, 4 (Fifth and Madison Aves.) to
53rd St.**

I hate to admit it, but sometimes I discover a delightful little pocket of city calm and I don't want to share it. I just want to keep it to myself. Such is the case with Paley Park.

This is not a park by suburban standards, but in midtown Manhattan you take whatever refuge you can get. An almost invisible oasis, Paley Park is situated in a concrete canyon sandwiched between two office buildings, complete with cascading twenty-five foot waterfall. Designed so visitors must step away from the continuity of the street line to enter the park, its offering of serenity is most fully appreciated as you walk past the potted junipers and approach the waterfall.

When you sit on the stone steps facing the falls, virtually all city sounds are muted by the resonant rumbling of the cascade. Add the visual play of the water and you have an experience that is deeply soothing and tranquilizing.

There's a small, lighted niche on each side of the falls that's easily accessible and particularly secluded. A refreshing mist bubbles up from the narrow catchment, and I have always found that nestling there intensifies the sense of calm.

Noontime note: A concession stand and patio-type furniture in the park accommodate business people and their bagged lunches. Between noon and 2 P.M. on nice days, it tends to get crowded. Skip those hours and you'll avoid a busy, although not unpleasant midday scene.

The Paramount Hotel Lobby

**Address: 235 West 43rd Street bet. Broadway
and Eighth Aves.
Phone: 764-5500
Hours: Daily, 24 Hours
Admission: Free
Subway: A, C, E, 1, 9, N, R to 42nd St.
Bus: M10 (Seventh and Eighth Aves.)
to 42nd St.**

If you want to get technical, hotel lobbies are not exactly public domain since they exist primarily for the comfort and service of their guests. But in practice, anyone who has spent time in this city can tell you of a favorite hotel lobby where he or she goes to meet friends and business associates, make a phone call, gather thoughts before an important meeting, or simply cop some quick relief from a city that can get in your face.

Good hotel lobbies are often easier to find than the best public atriums, and unless you are a particularly wacky dresser, or drag all your worldly possessions around in a grocery cart, you will not be asked to explain your presence there.

For me, one hotel lobby stands out above the rest — The Paramount. This fanciful space designed by Philippe Starck is just so cool. I love the hug-your-body-in-bold-velvet lounge chairs, the gray Venetian walls, the shadowy lighting, the over-hanging mezzanine restaurant. You might even bump into a Saturday Night Live host ("accom-modations for tonight's guests provided by ...").

I duck into other hotel lobbies for refuge, too, and no one's ever called the gendarmes: The Grand Hyatt (42nd St. and Lexington Avenue) offers a quick escape from the noisy netherworld of Grand Central Station. The upscale Four Seasons Hotel (57th Street between Park and Madison Avenues) and The New York Hilton (6th Avenue bet. 53rd and 54th Streets) offer both anonymity and elegant seating.

The Pier at Riverside South

**Address: Near 68th St. in Riverside Park/enter
at 72nd St.
Phone: (800) 201-PARK
Hours: Seven days, Dawn to dusk
Admission: Free
Subway: 1, 9 to 72nd St, walk five minutes
southwest
Bus: M5, M104 to 72nd St.**

I used to commute along the West Side Highway and from the elevated sections north of 59th Street, I would crane my neck for a glimpse at construction of the new pier at Riverside South. This waterside park seemed an inspired idea from the outset, as they spent months reinforcing the old maritime wharf, capping it with concrete, and laying down the circular shapes and swirling, whimsical brickwork that would form today's recreation-friendly site.

The Pier is just one of the highlights of a 21.5 acre Riverside South waterfront development that is returning miles of lost and neglected shoreline to the public. Eventually, plans call for a continuous esplanade around Manhattan Island that will link neighborhoods through an ambitious urban greenway system, including hundreds of miles of landscaped bike and pedestrian paths.

For the moment you can content yourself with this alluring jetty that thrusts 150 feet into the river, seeming to place you at the center of the Hudson River shipping lanes. Along the edges of this 40-foot wide pier you'll find dozens of bolted, wire mesh stadium seats pleasantly positioned to allow alternating views of the city skyline and silent river traffic. Here architects showed exceptional sensitivity of heart, an understanding of the romantic promise of the river, and the power of sonnets at sunset — most of the seating is in pairs, with plenty of distance between placements. Sweet.

Whether you live downtown, across town or out of town, make time for this waterfront retreat. Tell someone you care about that you know of a quiet place where you can speak softly, share secret longings, and hold hands securely. The Pier seems made for these intimate moments.

Poets
House

**Address: 72 Spring St. bet. Crosby and
Lafayette Sts., 2nd Floor
Phone: 431-7920
Hours: Tuesday through Friday, 11 A.M. to
7 P.M.; Saturday, 11 A.M. to
4 P.M.; Closed Sunday
Admission: Free
Subway: N or R to Prince St.; 6 to Spring St.
Bus: M1, 6 (Broadway) to Spring St.
Web site: www.poetshouse.org**

the French essayist and moralist, Joseph Joubert, once wrote, "You will not find poetry anywhere unless you bring some of it with you."

Actually, he was only partially correct. You'll find lots of poetry, for instance, at the Poets House, even if you leave yours at home. In fact, the genial staff has filled this comfortable, quiet, airy loft with more than 40,000 volumes of poetry — among the largest collection in the country that is open to the public.

Poetry has been enjoying a popular resurgence, treated like a newly discovered performance art on MTV and at local cafe readings. It's also been showing up on city buses and subways for years as part of the "Poetry In Motion" program, not to mention regular readings on NPR and public television. But the power of poetry is nothing new to the people at the Poets House. Here they've been well-versed (sorry) in promoting the value and richness of poetry since 1985 when poets Stanley Kunitz and Elizabeth Kray founded this sanctuary for sonnets and refuge for rhyme. Today it is an important literary resource center and a meeting place for poets worldwide.

Bathed in sunlight streaming in through several floor-to-ceiling windows, and tastefully furnished with colorfully upholstered reading chairs, Poets House is more a cozy living room than stuffy library. There is great respect for poetcraft here, and everyone is welcome.

Pratima
Ayurvedic Clinic

**Address: 162 West 56th St., Suite 204, bet.
Sixth and Seventh Aves.
Phone: 581-8136
Hours: Tuesday, Thursday and Friday, 10 A.M.
to 6:30 P.M.; Wednesday
10 A.M. to 6 P.M.; Saturday 10 A.M. to 4 P.M.;
Closed Sunday and Monday
Admission: $65 for one hour Facial
Subway: N, R to 57th St.
Bus: M5 (Sixth Ave.) to 57th St.**

a t a small, unpretentious skin-care salon near
Carnegie Hall, hundreds of New Yorkers have
discovered a 5000-year-old formula for rejuvenating both their outer selves and inner spirits.
Basing its treatments on Ayurveda – an ancient
Indian discipline considered the "mother science
of healing" – the Pratima Clinic has quietly
emerged as the city's leading center for
traditional Ayurvedic treatments.

The 20-year-old Pratima Clinic is the creation of
Dr. Pratima Raichur. She pioneered the use of
Ayurveda in the U.S., and simply sitting near this

gracious woman has a soothing effect on the entire body. Receiving her gentle treatments in the serene surroundings of the Pratima Clinic, however, introduces you to an even more subtle state of bliss.

I have been a devotee of Pratima's Aromatherapy Facial for more than a decade, and it's one of the nicest things you will ever do for your face. Pratima emphasizes that inner stress manifests outwardly as unhealthy skin, so at Pratima they work to bring all the senses into proper balance. The soft green and pink walls of the recently renovated treatment rooms calm the mind, Indian chanting music opens the heart, and the hypnotic aroma of Pratima's herbal tinctures and essential oils work their magic on the olfactory sense.

Maybe I'm hallucinating, but I always feel my skin looks years younger after an hour at Pratima. And, best of all, my restored sense of inner peace doesn't wash off.

The Quad at Columbia University

Address: 116th St. and Broadway
Hours: Daily, 8 A.M. to 6 P.M.
Admission: Free
Subway: 1, 9 to 116th St.
Bus: M4, M11, M104 (Broadway) to 116th St.

Leaving the tumult of Broadway to wander into the main quad at Columbia is like transferring from the schoolroom of urban survival to a restful course on personal revival.

The safest grounds in New York (big league security for busy Ivy Leaguers) are also a mecca for academic activity and reclusive repose. There's no need to worry about your age or how you're dressed, either — people just assume you're a graduate student or an esteemed university professor strolling the quad.

Relaxation 101 is self-taught every day in front of the Low Library, where you can nestle against the easternmost corner of that noble twelve-foot wall. It's a warm, windless nook excellent for studying the campus goings-on. Carry a book — cerebral reading is a popular pastime for all who recline on the broad lawns.

You might prefer the smaller, less-frequented quad in front of Uris Hall (look for the "Curl" sculpture of twisted black tubes). Or amble through the maze of century-old buildings until you find your own solitary spot. There are a dozen on this postcard-perfect campus where you can partake of the scholarly atmosphere undisturbed.

My final evaluation: the Columbia University quad is a high-spirited, unhurried place for intel-lectual and physical renewal. I give it an A.

Robert F. Wagner Jr. Park

Address: Battery Place and West Street
Phone: 416-5300
Hours: Daily, dawn to dusk
Admission: Free
Subway: R to Battery Park; 6 to Bowling Green; 1 to South Ferry
Bus: M1, 6 (Broadway) to State St.

good green grass isn't easy to find in New York. I'm talking about the really dense, carpet-thick stuff that's not trampled thin by soccer cleats, littered with cigarette butts, or dotted with dog doody — the kind of lush covering you can lie on, letting your tension seep into the body of the earth.

The best public expanse of green grass in the city is at the spectacular Robert Wagner Park, tucked between the Museum of Jewish Heritage and Battery Park in lower Manhattan. A masterfully designed wedge of land jutting into the lower harbor, there is simply no better place to

watch passing river traffic while comfortably
sprawled over soft turf.

A team of urban horticulturists has transformed
acres of landfill here into perhaps the finest dis-
play garden anywhere in New York. A vibrant
palette of perennials and annuals explodes from
dozens of carefully organized tree pits and
planting beds, all casting sweet perfumes across
the manicured lawns. Those flawless lawns are
preserved without herbicides and pesticides
either. They practice a strict philosophy of landscape maintenance here that eschews the use of
toxic chemicals. So you can pluck a blade of
grass and nibble on it with no harmful side
effects.

I like to ride my bike to Robert Wagner early in
the morning. I pick a spot on the northern lawn,
stare out at the best harbor views in Manhattan,
and let the blanket of soft blades under my back
turn me all warm and wistful. That good green
grass — Mother Earth's natural tranquilizer.

st. Luke's Garden

Address: Hudson St. between Barrow and Grove Sts.
Phone: 924-0562
Hours: Tuesday through Friday, 8 A.M. to dusk.; Saturday and Sunday, 8 A.M. to dusk
Admission: Free
Subway: 1, 9 to Sheridan Square, walk west
Bus: M10 (Seventh and Eighth Aves.) to Christopher St.

for anyone who grew up in the suburbs, one of the great memories of childhood was having a backyard.

You knew there was a fast-paced world rushing past your front door, but out back, life was easy and innocent and fun. The backyard was a far-away place to hide in a daydream, to stare at the sky, or to simply forget.

St. Luke's Garden is the closest thing to having your own backyard in New York City. In fact, it actually is the backyard for several handsome nineteenth- century brownstones that enclose the secret garden on two sides. For years I'd peer behind the wall at St. Luke's, envious of whoever had access to this apparently private spot. Turns out all my peering was pointless; the obscured public gate wasn't far away. You enter this green oasis by passing under the gold and white sign on Hudson St. that reads "St. Luke's School." Follow the footpath west, then south through the quaint schoolyard until you reach the welcoming garden gate.

Splendidly concealed behind an ivy-blanketed brick wall, the garden feels well-removed from the Village activity which surrounds it. The mandala-like design of its stone pathways and the thoughtfully placed magnolia-hidden benches contribute to a sense of "backyard" privacy. St. Luke's Garden is a neat retreat in winter, too, when its dormant foliage is a study in tones of gray, brown, green and red.

St. Patrick's Cathedral

Address: Fifth Ave. between 50th and 51st Sts.
Phone: 753-2261
Hours: Daily, 7:30 A.M. to 9:30 P.M.
Admission: Free
Subway: E, F to 53rd St.; B, D, F to
Rockefeller Center
Bus: M1, 2, 3, 4 (Fifth and Madison Aves.) to
50th St.

new York has so many magnificent churches, synagogues, and religious centers, all conducive to inner contemplation and quiet, it is difficult to single out just one.

St. Patrick's Cathedral would certainly have to be counted among the most beautiful, however, with its twin Gothic spires reaching 330 feet above the street. The cathedral's cavernous interior seats 2400 people, houses an organ with more than 7380 pipes, and contains some of the most breathtaking stained glass in the world.

And you don't have to be searching for salvation to benefit from the cathedral's ready gift of peace and quiet. With acres of polished wooden pews, there is always an isolated corner in which to escape. I particularly enjoy the altars to saints, which you'll find by walking past the pulpit at the east end of the cathedral. I'm always amazed to find so much solitude just steps from Fifth Avenue, and smack in the middle of Manhattan.

For those who can't conveniently get to St. Patrick's, I think you'll find these spiritual sanctuaries to be equally sustaining: Grace Church (Broadway and 10th Street), Marble Collegiate Church (Fifth Avenue and 29th Street), Temple Emanu-El (Fifth Avenue and 65th Street), and the Cathedral of St. John the Divine (W. 112th Street and Amsterdam Avenue).

Snug Harbor
Cultural Center

Address: 1000 Richmond Terrace, Staten Island
Phone: (718) 448-2500
Hours: Daily, 9 A.M. to 5 P.M.
Admission: Free
Bus: From Staten Island Ferry, take S40 direct-
ly to Snug Harbor (two miles)
Auto: Verrazano Bridge (lower level), to first
exit on Bay St., to Snug Harbor
Web site: www.snug-harbor.org

Whenever I'm at Snug Harbor, I catch myself glancing around for leathery-faced guys with peg legs and eye patches. This former retirement community for "aged, decrepit, and worn out sailors," hasn't served that function in many years; it's just that the entire eighty acres of parklands, Greek Revival buildings and Victorian cottages look so much like they did back in the 1880s.

Snug Harbor was purchased by the City of New York in 1976, but restoration of this relic to its nautical heyday is a slow process that progresses in spurts as funds appear. Still, the nationally landmarked historic district overlooking New York Bay is a fascinating place to explore.

For a delightfully creepy experience, walk down the old funeral march road (Cottage Row) where deceased sailors were escorted to their graves. This processional path leads to remote sections of the wooded grounds, then loops back past a large pond lined with willows, wetlands, and the English-style perennial gardens maintained by the Staten Island Botanical Gardens. Snug Harbor remains a bit of buried treasure, a well-kept secret from both sea and land-bound publics. Even if you're not an old salt, do set sail for historic Snug Harbor.

Traveler's Note: As a fast growing center for the arts, Snug Harbor offers a year-round program of music concerts, dance recitals, art exhibits, and workshops. Call ahead about upcoming events.

South
Cove

Address: South End Ave. at Battery Park City
Hours: Daily, 24 hours
Admission: Free
Subway: 1, 9, A, E to Chambers Street, walk
west, then south past World Financial Center
Bus: M10 (Eighth Ave.) to Battery Park City

Whenever I approach this playful inlet, it begins to work its primal magic, reminding me instantly how much and how often I long to be near water.

It is not surprising that South Cove should have this effect, since everything about it — from the boulder-studded boardwalk and bowed bridge to the arching jetty and crown-like observation deck — is designed to get people back to the shoreline. For too many decades, the Hudson waterfront here was rendered inaccessible by a frustrating barrier of decaying wharves and razor-wire-topped fences. Reclaiming this neglected landscape for refuge-starved New Yorkers is precisely what artists and architects had uppermost in their minds when they conceived South Cove.

You can see, smell, even feel the surge of the river from any point along the curving architecture of this sheltered recess. The harmonious sounds of its swirling eddies call you to the water's edge. And the three-acre coastal park overflows with sunny seats, too; try out the rail-tie benches against the south-facing wall, which stay cozily warm even in winter.

The extremely safe, always quiet South Cove reveals its most compelling feature at night, when cobalt blue ship's lanterns turn the nook into a romantic fantasyland. This is the precious, whispering light of the heart — bring along a special friend.

Strawberry Fields

Address: Central Park West at 72nd St.
Hours: Daily, Dawn to dusk
Admission: Free
Subway: B or C to 72nd St.
**Bus: M10 (Seventh and Eighth Aves.) to 72nd
St.; M72 (72nd St. crosstown) to Central Park
West**

a t the entrance to Strawberry Fields, a sign reads "Reserved for Quiet Recreation." While New Yorkers may be less than fanatical in their observance of these posted notices, their devotion to Beatle icon John Lennon is quite another matter.

Located across the street from the Dakota, where Yoko Ono still resides, this four-and-a-half acre living memorial to Lennon created by his wife seems to be permanently imbued with the spirit of the Sixties. Once you step over the black and white "Imagine" mosaic embedded in the foot-path leading to Strawberry Fields, you feel just a bit more hopeful — much like we did back then. The first thing you'll notice about this idyllic setting is that it's scrupulously cared for, thanks to private funds earmarked for its upkeep. Sun-dappled and friendly in every season, the planted flower beds and grassy knolls get daily, almost constant attention.

You won't have any trouble finding breathing space here, but you can treat yourself to a particularly quieting experience by walking to the northernmost end of the upper lawn where it comes to an abrupt point. See that single redwood tree in front of the hedge line? Under that tree I fed a sparrow a piece of bread from my hand. Imagine.

Sutton Place Park

Address: Sutton Place at 57th St.
Hours: Daily, Dawn to dusk
Admission: Free
Subway: 4, 5, 6 to 59th St., walk east.
Bus: M15 (First and Second Aves.) to 57th St.

the most rejuvenating urban parks are those with a distinct feeling of detachment from the noise and turbulence of the city.

The physical design of Sutton Place Park makes it just such a soothing setting. A three-foot retaining wall and an eight-foot drop from street level completely conceal this park from Sutton Place and 57th Street. But it's there, tucked between a stately brownstone and a tall residential building. Just descend the switch-back ramp and you'll enter a friendly and protected realm.

At first, your gaze settles on Porcellino, the life-sized wild boar (a replica of a beloved bronze sculpture in Florence, Italy) who patiently and imposingly presides over this quiet park. Next, your eyes are drawn to the movement of the East River — the park's visual focal point. If you stand near the edge of the quadrangle and look down, you have the feeling you're suspended over swirling waters. This evokes the pleasant sensation of riding atop the river currents, and lures the mind away from outer-world intrusions.

Sutton Place is one of the city's most exclusive neighborhoods and as a result, its park enjoys excellent police protection. Visitors here are genteel and respectful, the atmosphere is sedate, and you'll ascend the ramp to the real world with renewed equanimity.

United Nations
Garden

Address: First Ave. at 45th St.
Phone: 963-1234
Hours: Daily, 9 A.M. to 5 P.M.
Admission: Free; no food or drink allowed
Subway: 4, 5, 6 to Grand Central, walk east
Bus: M15 (First and Second Aves.) to 42nd St.;
M42 (42nd St. crosstown)
to First Ave.
Web site: www.un.org

While the United Nations is a favorite stop for foreign tourists, New Yorkers routinely overlook this monument to global brotherhood. Look again, because just north of the UN's celebrated glass and concrete Secretariat building is an expansive, under-utilized garden providing the perfect urban getaway.

Within the UN's sixteen acres of grounds and garden, you'll find 1400 prize-winning rosebushes, 185 flowering cherry trees, fifty-two dwarf fruit trees, plus ambling walkways, strategically placed benches, and a half-mile paved esplanade offering spectacular views of the East River. This is truly a walkway of the world, with a mosaic of smiling faces from almost every country on earth assuring you that global peace is still possible. Guarded by UN security, the entire area is also extremely safe.

Whenever I'm there, I quickly gravitate towards the Eleanor Roosevelt Memorial in the north-east corner of the garden. It's tucked away behind a small stand of trees and from the seclusion of its huge stone bench you can while away an entire afternoon. Or even doze undisturbed. I know. I have.

Traveler's Note: Be sure to see the twisted-pistol sculpture at the 45th Street entrance to the garden. How safe our city would be if every firearm looked as useless as this one.

Wave Hill

Address: 675 West 252nd St., Bronx
Phone: (718) 549-3200
Hours: Tuesday through Sunday, 9 A.M. to
5:30 P. M. (4:30 P.M. Winter);
closed Monday
Admission: $4
Subway/Bus: Call for directions
Auto: Henry Hudson Pkwy. to 246-250th St.,
north to 252nd St., follow signs to Wave Hill
Web site: www.wavehill.org

Ladies and gentlemen, may I present your country estate.

All right, all right, not your country estate, but a country estate, and you're invited to come up here anytime you like and use it.

Currently owned by the city, Wave Hill in the Riverdale section of the Bronx recalls a time when former residents Teddy Roosevelt, Mark Twain, and Arturo Toscanini called it their weekend retreat. Today it offers nature-deprived cityfolk a verdant escape just twenty minutes from Manhattan. The twenty-eight acres of glorious gardens, a cluster of greenhouses, sweeping lawns, lily pond, and unspoiled woodlands occupy a hilltop that brings you face-to-face with The Palisades — a geologic wonder that never fails to astonish.

The mansion contains a gift shop and café with outdoor seating, as well as a children's arts and environmental education center. There's also plenty of clean air and open land at Wave Hill and lots of inviting spots to turn your back on a tight and toxic city. Many gravitate toward the rough-hewn gazebo in the Wild Garden, but I'm partial to the high-backed lawn chairs generously distributed throughout the grounds. Bring your watercolors. You might be inspired to paint soothing, soft-hued pictures of your, uh, country estate to hang on your city walls.

World Financial Center

Address: West Street, between the West Side Highway and the Hudson River
Phone: 945-0505
Hours: Daily, 6 A.M. to Midnight
Admission: Free
Subway: 1, 9, A, E to Chambers Street, walk west and south to World Financial Center
Bus: M10 (7th and 8th Aves.) to Battery Park City
Web site: www.worldfinancialcenter.com

September 11, 2001 changed the landscape of Manhattan's south end forever. Despite great loss and destruction, the riverfront refuge on the west side of the World Financial Center remained relatively intact and, today, continues to offer a wealth of waterside peace and quiet.

It's well worth investing time here, as the financial visionaries of Wall Street spent a small fortune on a wharf-like mall that is not only spectacular to look at but was also purposefully

designed to be a haven for frazzled
money managers.

Here are my three favorite spots: (1) the pink
granite benches below and in front of the "quota-
tion" fence facing the man-made cove (you'll
know it when you see it); (2) the circle of wood-
en benches in the maze garden at the southeast
corner of the mall; (3) the broad promenade that
begins at the southwest corner of the cove.
Although not technically part of the Financial
Center, this bench-lined walkway which extends
nearly to Battery Park has river views and
romance to rival Paris. It's well lit and safe at
night, too.

Many visit this area now with powerful memories
of the tragedy. If you bring your own intentions
for outer and inner peace, and make a deposit of
that healing energy as you sit adjacent to the
World Financial Center, then others can draw
from the fund of friendship and understanding
that has accumulated here.

15 More Great Urban Sanctuaries...

because you can
never have enough
peace and quiet.

Battery Park

It has served as an inviting public space for more than 200 years, and Battery Park is still a qualified haven from the pressures of the nearby Financial District. Named for the battery of cannons originally placed here to guard Manhattan (Castle Clinton, an early nineteenth-century fort, still remains), the park has sun and seagulls, a wide riverfront esplanade, 180 degree water views, and miles of bench-lined pathways. For maximum privacy I retreat to the shadow of the huge stone monoliths comprising the East Coast War Memorial, where there always seems to be a seat, even at lunch hour, when overstressed Wall Streeters stream into the park to regain composure and perspective. And don't forget the nearby Staten Island Ferry — the free, 50-minute round-trip cruise is still the best way to see the glittering Lower Manhattan skyline.

The **Bell Tower** at
Riverside Church

**Address: 490 Riverside Drive at 120th St.
Phone: 870-6700**

I know why Quasimodo took refuge in a bell tower — the privacy, the views, and those great big beautiful bells. At a height of 392 feet, this Gothic belfry is one of the world's tallest, offering unobstructed perspectives on New York and New Jersey. It also houses seventy-four carillon bells ranging in size from a twenty-ton bronze behemoth — the largest tuned bell ever cast — to a dainty ten-pounder. I suggest climbing the steps through the maze of bells to the narrow, outdoor observation deck. From here the vistas are giddily inspiring, and when the bells toll on the hour, you can scream as loud as you want without being arrested. After a major 2001 renovation, the Sunday carillon recitals continue, attracting a small, devoted crowd looking for a good head ringing.

Bloom

**Address: 16 W. 21 St., bet. Fifth and
Sixth Aves.
Phone: 620-5666**

Try walking past Bloom without going inside.
The sidewalk topiaries in front of this unique
flower shop call you over. Bundles of vines dan-
gling from the roof reach out to you. Vases full of
cut flowers in the entranceway whisper for your
attention. Everything about Bloom encourages
you to step off the street for a quick breather.
Bloom, housed in an old, single-story Chelsea
storefront with bare brick walls and thick wood
ceiling rafters, is so pretty to look at, you'll eager-
ly pause for its refreshment. Visiting the East
Village? Step into another sweet floral design
shop, Cottage Garden (225 E. 5th Street), where
genial owner, Yuki, will serve you tea as you
browse among her exquisite dried flower
arrangements.

Brooklyn Botanic Garden

Address: 1000 Washington Ave., Brooklyn
Phone: (718) 623-7200   Web site:
www.bbg.org

Few places offer such a total package of rest and refreshment as the horticulturally varied Brooklyn Botanic Garden. This 52-acre palette of ever-changing color and beauty is as diverse as the many surrounding cultures it serves. Two destinations top my list here. The traditional Japanese Hill-and-Pond Garden is a secluded arcadia, highlighted by a meandering pond where you can watch the colorful koi loll through still waters. Walk around the pond to the second tier of waterfalls where small grottos in the rock create a soothing aural tapestry of overlapping echoes. At the Fragrance Garden, you're encouraged to rub the leaves of plants both obscure and familiar. On the tips of your fingers, you'll capture hints of lemon and mint, fennel and lavender — dozens of inviting essences which trigger a lifetime of remembrances.

Cornelia St. Cafe's
Fireplace Room

**Address: 29 Cornelia St. bet. Bleecker and
W. 4th St.
Phone: 989-9319**

What is it about a fireplace that can turn a difficult day into a forgiving one, or make an uncertain world seem less frightening? It's a question best considered in front of a blazing winter hearth, a light snow falling, a mug of tea clasped securely between your hands. They have a cozy fireplace in the backroom at the Cornelia St. Cafe — with a charred brick face, a stack of chunky hardwoods alongside, and the sound of crackling logs thawing the air. This is a fine, secluded place to snuggle with a friend, where the tea is served piping hot and they let you linger leisurely over dinner. Another spot to warm your toes during the cold months is The Ye Waverly Inn (16 Bank Street), an 1844 carriage house with cozy wooden booths where they always keep a log on the fire for you.

General Society Library

Address: 20 W. 44 St. bet. Fifth and Sixth Aves.
Phone: 921-1767

I was sitting below the enormous skylight in the main reading room of the General Society Library looking out the front door at some passing trucks. I could see them, but I couldn't hear them — it was like the soundtrack was missing. That's what's so cool about this oak-trimmed member library — it's so quiet, you can't believe you're in the city, much less in the heart of midtown. Founded in 1820, this marble-pillared depository of 140,000 volumes (many on things mechanical) is housed in a stately nineteenth-century structure that looks off-limits to tradeless folks like me. But the private library is open to casual visitors, who are welcome to study, browse, or bask in the remarkable silence. You'll marvel over this miracle of muted sound.

Housing Works
Used Book Cafe

Address: 126 Crosby St., bet. Houston and Prince Sts.
Phone: 334-3324

It is in bookstores like this one that literary New York are born: walls lined floor to ceiling with mahogany bookcases; tables piled high with tempting titles; comfy, overstuffed chairs where you can read three chapters of a relished novel before deciding to buy it; a relaxed atmosphere where the works of great writers can be lingered over, not rushed through. This antiquarian treasure trove in SoHo specializes in unusual and out-of-print books, with a fine selection of art and drama titles. Balconies lined with more and equally enticing tomes run along opposite sides of the shop, giving it the feel of a funky, old, New York bookshop, a browser's paradise, where you can find Balzac's complete works, or the like, tucked away on a high shelf. Wear a watch — you're in danger of losing entire afternoons here.

The Jefferson Market Garden

Address: Greenwich Avenue between 9th and 10th Sts.

As thrill-seeking New Yorkers, we tend to glorify intensity and excitement. We want everything bigger and more sensational. But the serenity-seeker dwelling inside us asks that we consider the city on a smaller scale, that we take periodic refuge in a quieter, simpler New York. The quaint Jefferson Market Garden sits unobtrusively behind a high wrought iron fence in the center of Greenwich Village. From May through October (every day except Monday), you can sidestep the city and slip into the garden's unhurried charms. This little haven, resplendent with flourishing color in the growing seasons, is designed to stimulate interest in horticulture and the environment. Just follow the red brick road that snakes gently through the garden and breathe deeply. Exhale slowly. And remember life's little wonders.

Liz Christy Bowery-Houston Garden

Address: Northeast corner of Houston and
Bowery Sts.
Phone: 594-2155
Web site: www.greenguerillas.org

"Fueled by volunteer energy, a commitment to the earth, and neighborhood pride," reads the motto of the Liz Christy Garden. It could apply to any of the city's 700-plus community gardens, but in 1973, activist Liz Christy and her resident band of Green Guerillas were the first to successfully reclaim a rubble-strewn lot and return it to a fertile place for growing and gardening. Today volunteers regularly till, weed and water the sixty beds bursting with vegetables, fruit trees, and fragrant herbs. I am always amazed at how a trio of birch trees and a low ridge of thick wildflowers can buffer the sounds of Houston Street traffic. It's easy to see why locals flock here for quick encounters with nature, whether to stare at the small pond or pluck grapes from the simple trellis.

Shakespeare Garden

Tucked in the shadow of the Belvedere Castle in Central Park, just a stone's throw from the Delacorte Theater where Shakespearean performances rule the summer, this shady, texturally enticing garden is a romantic place. Its tightly coiled flagstone paths serpentine up a short hill to a secluded circle of grass — a favorite spot for early evening picnickers bound for the theater. But it's the garden itself — overflowing with more than 120 plants cultivated from seeds and cuttings taken directly from Shakespeare's garden in Stratford-upon-Avon — that is most enchanting. There is no way to walk through it quickly — the placement of the spiraling steps almost forbids it. But what's your hurry? Take in the delphiniums, ferns and delicate poppies, and waste lots of time here. Your soul will be eternally grateful.

The **Shearwater**

Address: The Harbor at World Financial Center
Phone: Toll-Free (800) 544-1224

Surrounded as we are by concrete and steel in the abysmal gray canyons of Manhattan, we can forget that we're living on an island. And islands are surrounded by large bodies of, yes, water, just perfect for sailing. The mariners who own The Shearwater, a vintage 1929 Maine schooner, haven't forgotten.

They invite you along as they navigate through lower Hudson Harbor where you can enjoy heartstopping views of old Manhattan and the Big Green Lady. Call for reservations from mid May through October on the relaxing lunchtime sail (about $18 per person/one hour), the sunset cruise (about $30/two hours), or the wind-in-your-hair evening rejuvenator (about $35/two hours). This pristine 82-foot yacht, with its handsome teak decks and billowing sails will work wonders on your stress, surrounding you with sea spray and serenity during an exhilarating offshore mini-vacation.

Vera List Courtyard at The New School

Address: 65 West 11th St., east of Sixth Ave.

The enthusiasm of students never fails to recharge and reassure me. This positive energy seems magnified at The New School where 70-year old matriculators coexist with classmates a third their age. I like this kind of intergenerational mingling — it's good for the soul. And you can participate anytime by visiting the Vera List Courtyard — a progressive fusion of wood, stone and steel which links the two New School buildings. Sign in at the guard's desk to access this imaginative community courtyard and micro-campus, furnished with three mortar-and-pestle-style circular benches, one of rock maple, another of granite, and a third of mesh steel. They're fun to sit on for mindless musing, but it's the gently sloping, circular walkway that spirals up to a cinder mound that I employ for slow meditative walks. No chance of sagging spirits here.

Washington Mews

Walk slowly. No, slower. As slowly as you'd walk
if you were holding the hand of a two-year-old.
There, that's the perfect pace for strolling this
nineteenth-century cobblestone alleyway in
Greenwich Village. I live only two blocks from
the Washington Mews and never miss a chance
to amble snail-like through this narrow lane,
which bisects a block of two-story structures
built as stables and carriage houses in the 1830s.
Nestled within the campus grid of New York
University, the mews is well patrolled and always
safe. At one time, at least a half a dozen of these
private back streets were open to pedestrians
who wanted to detour off busier thoroughfares
into more peaceful passageways. Now only a few
remain unlocked. So get here while you still can
and, remember, slow down.

The Water Tunnel at 48th Street

Address: 48th to 49th Sts., bet. Sixth and Seventh Aves.

Sometimes you have to slip into the cracks of the city to find precious places for peace and privacy. The pass-through plaza between 48th and 50th Streets — with a mesmerizing glass water tunnel as its centerpiece — is a wedge of serenity in Manhattan's tight architecture. For years I would rush past the narrow opening to this plaza and be surprised by its sudden presence. Now I seek out the slim passageway specifically to walk through the water tunnel — a Plexiglas opening about 15-feet-long with a slate bridge down its middle and water cascading over it from a waterfall above. A walk through the water tube takes just seconds, but it is calming and pleasant, nevertheless. Children can never pass through without stopping to look up and stare. The tunnel's light mists will have the same captivating effect on the child inside you.

West Side Community Garden

Address: 89th and 90th Sts., bet. Columbus and Amsterdam Aves.
Web site: www.westsidecommunitygarden.org

Folks who find freedom in fresh air and flourishing flora will want to make regular stops at this community garden — a remarkable tribute to the sweat of local residents, who battle developers to retain green open space forever. There are two distinct areas of this garden: an upper section with 80 private plots producing bountiful crops of zucchini, eggplant and tomatoes; and the lower garden which is designed for public use and is distinguished by three concentric circles rimmed with comfortable wooden benches and well-manicured border plantings. Resplendent with 13,000 tulips during the spring Tulip Festival, this area is where neighbors gather to celebrate the victory of crocuses over concrete.

Index

About
the Author

Allan Ishac is an advertising copywriter and ·creator of the Telly Award-winning Hard Hat Harry™ children's video series. He is also the author of *New York's 50 Best Places To Take Children*, and editor of *50 Best Places to Keep Your Spirit Alive*. Allan lives in Manhattan and seeks serenity through balloon sculpting.